TRUMPET

CD INCLUDED

HAL•LEONARD
**BIG BAND PLAY-ALONG
VOLUME 2**

Popular Hits

ISBN-13: 978-1-4234-2229-7
ISBN-10: 1-4234-2229-5

**HAL•LEONARD®
CORPORATION**

7777 W. BLUEMOUND RD. P.O. BOX 13819 MILWAUKEE, WI 53213

Visit Hal Leonard Online at
www.halleonard.com

CD INCLUDED

HAL•LEONARD
BIG BAND
PLAY-ALONG
VOLUME 2

Popular Hits

AIN'T NO MOUNTAIN HIGH ENOUGH

Trumpet

Words and Music by
NICKOLAS ASHFORD and VALERIE SIMPSON
Arranged by ROGER HOLMES

BRICK HOUSE

Trumpet

Words and Music by LIONEL RICHIE, RONALD LaPREAD,
WALTER ORANGE, MILAN WILLIAMS,
THOMAS McCLARY and WILLIAM KING
Arranged by PAUL MURTHA

TRUMPET

COPACABANA
(At The Copa)

Trumpet

Words by BRUCE SUSSMAN and JACK FELDMAN
Music by BARRY MANILOW
Arranged by JOHN BERRY

Recorded by SANTANA

EVIL WAYS

Words and Music by SONNY HENRY
Arranged by ROGER HOLMES

TRUMPET

TRUMPET

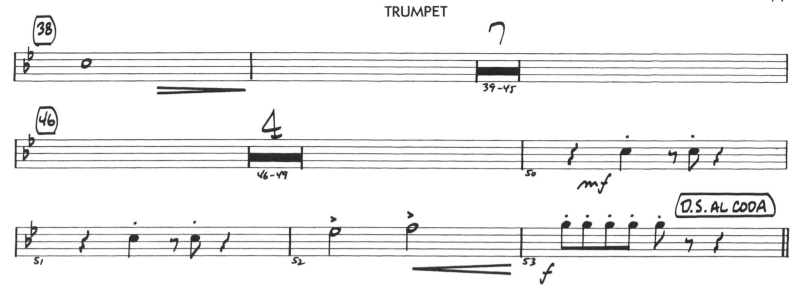

I HEARD IT THROUGH THE GRAPEVINE

Trumpet

Words and Music by
NORMAN J. WHITFIELD and BARRETT STRONG
Arranged by JOHN BERRY

TRUMPET

Recorded by GEORGE BENSON

on broadway

Words and Music by
**BARRY MANN, CYNTHIA WEIL,
MIKE STOLLER** and **JERRY LEIBER**
Arranged by JOHN HIGGINS

Recorded by ARETHA FRANKLIN

RESPECT

Words and Music by
OTIS REDDING

Arranged by PAUL MURTHA

Trumpet

TRUMPET

This page intentionally left blank

STREET LIFE

Trumpet

Words and Music by
WILL JENNINGS and JOE SAMPLE
Arranged by RICK STITZEL

YESTERDAY

Trumpet

Words and Music by
JOHN LENNON and PAUL McCARTNEY
Arranged by JOHN BERRY

TRUMPET

Recorded by THE CHERRY POPPIN' DADDIES

ZOOT SUIT RIOT

Trumpet

Words and Music by STEVE PERRY
Arranged by PAUL MURTHA

TRUMPET